WHAT YOU NEED TO READ TO KNOW JUST ABOUT EVERYTHING

WHAT YOU NEED TO READ TO KNOW JUST ABOUT EVERYTHING

The 25 best books for a self education and why

Allen L. Scarbrough

Writers Club Press

San Jose New York Lincoln Shanghai

What You Need To Read To Know Just About Everything
The 25 best books for a self education and why

Writers Club Press
an imprint of iUniverse, Inc.

For information address:
iUniverse, Inc.
5220 S. 16th St., Suite 200
Lincoln, NE 68512
www.iuniverse.com

All books were selected by the author. All commentary is the opinion of the author only.

ISBN: 0-595-24315-0

CONTENTS

▼

INTRODUCTION

▼

Hello, and welcome to my world. The purpose of this book is to save you an incredible amount of time and energy in the struggle to become a person of learning. Some of us went to college, but came out of the experience lacking sophistication. Some of us skipped the whole experience and went straight to the job market, but now we are longing for a little of the finer things in life. In short, we all desire to be "well read" yet few of us are. The problem is time, where on God's earth do we get the time to become a person of learning? I will offer some examples of how to make the time available before we get into the books.

First let me introduce myself and tell you why I feel qualified and able to write this type of book. I am first and foremost a voracious reader; forget that, I eat voracious readers for lunch. I lost count some years ago but have read somewhere in the vicinity of two thousand five hundred books. Some were easy reads, such as <u>Jonathon Livingston Seagull,</u> all the way up to the holy grail of books the 1483 pages of tiny print that is <u>War and Peace.</u> I have also written three previous books. What I want to accomplish in this book is to set out for you the 25 best and most worthwhile books to read so that even a person with limited time and energy can become "well read" in one year setting aside one to two hours a day. This pace allows you two weeks per book. Some books will require a few days, others a month.

Now I already hear you whining from clear across the country in Oregon. I don't have an hour or two a day. Yes you do and I'm going to show you where it's hiding. But first let me set out my criteria for the books I have chosen. First, does the book lend insight into a particular culture, era, or people? Second, does the book offer unique insights or is it just a rehash of information available in many other places? Third, does the book examine the human condition in a way that is useful to most people? And fourth and last, is the book a vigorous and engaging read or is it dull as nails. I hope to save you hours and hours of boredom slogging through boring and redundant manuscripts that I myself have had to endure. Consider it the price I had to pay for the money you spent on this book. I truly believe that I can turn you from a "cultural illiterate" into a shining "literary star" in one year. And I offer this money back guarantee. If you read this book and follow its program and do not feel that you have become among the literary elite then I guarantee that when you write a better book on the same subject I will buy it. How's that?

The next issue to address is why read 25 books in one year. The most obvious reason is that people who have read great books are looked up to in this society and are considered "learned." I can't tell you how amazed people have been to find out I have actually read War and Peace. They look at me as if I am some sort of minor god for although they have intended many times to read such works of art they have only seen the movie versions. So, besides status and admiration, the second thing you will acquire is a sense of history.

Why go around in life repeating all the dumb mistakes of your for-bearers when a simple reading of their times can show you the folly of your current path.

But the biggest and best reason for following this program is the immense pleasure of touching some of the finest art and most profound thinking that man has created. These books will enrich your life in ways unimaginable and make of you a person of substance. I hope you will truly read these great works and conclude with me at the end that you have been made wiser, more able, more compassionate and in turn more employable than you thought possible. Here's to the incredible journey you are about to make and to greeting you on the other side of these books in the holy land of knowledge.

READING TIME AND TIPS

We are all busy creatures. The bane of our modern existence is that all of our labor saving devices have done little except trap us into ungodly modes of living, perhaps out of a suitcase or worse, a mini-van. Yet despite all the distractions there is time to complete the reading of these twenty-five books in one year. However, take as long a period of time as you need. I do believe that completing these books in one year will produce the greatest personal transformation, but I would much rather you read them period than that you gave up due to time constraints. And as a note of caution, I'm not a moralist in the anal retentive mode. Some of these books do contain sexual images, scenes and descriptions, but I will not save you from what these words have to teach. So be forewarned.

Reading is considered by some as a luxury of time. To me this is ludicrous; reading is as essential as water and oxygen. Without the ability to read and to touch other lives and thoughts we are little more than victims of our own prejudices. To become a citizen of the world requires applied thought and concern. Reading gives the heart and mind the impetus to effect these changes. Do not get discouraged or dismayed at the daunting task of opening an eight hundred-page book and thinking there is no way you can ever wade through it. I have a very short attention span and made my way to the other side of many excellent, but long, books. I offer you some tips to get you started.

First and foremost the best time to read is right as you get into bed for the night. You may fall asleep in fifteen minutes or half an hour, but that is perfectly fine. You can probably read five to ten of the smaller books on this list in just these few minutes before sleep. As an added bonus you will fall asleep more quickly. Secondly, we all have business to attend in the bathroom daily or almost daily. Keep at least one of the books on the list by the toilet for perusing when nature calls. I suggest you pick one that is broken up into small chapters so that thoughts can be more easily recaptured.

But without a doubt the secret to keeping going is to be reading at least three books at a time. I can't tell you how many books I have read one or two pages at a time. What this does is prevent a slow section of a book from bogging down the whole plan. If you have three books going and one is interesting to you then read that book last and start with a book that is going through a "slow" period and read only one to three pages, whatever you can stand. You will amaze yourself at your ability to read even a book that you consider boring or slow. Hopefully, few of these books will be difficult to finish. That indeed is the very purpose of this book, to weed out the unnecessary, the dull, the profane, the non-amusing, the ill informing, the oft repeating and the plain old banal.

I believe wholeheartedly in the books that I recommend. I ask you to trust a reader of the first order in your quest toward literary enlightenment. There are few endeavors in life that can compare to the feeling of being able to discourse with educated people and to be taken seriously in their company. I challenge you to give this book to others you feel will benefit from it after you are done. But please buy them their own copy as this is a reference book. I offer in parting three words of advice, read, read, read.

SIDDHARTHA

I want to point out at the start that these books are in no particular order. Feel free to jump around in any manner you wish. Reading, to me, is an exercise just like any other physical activity and I suggest a short, easy to read book to start off with. <u>Siddhartha</u> by German novelist Herman Hesse is a short book about the life of a young man living in the time of Buddha. It is neither dogmatic nor preachy, but indeed is a book primarily about the wanderings of a great soul and how he comes to meet the Buddha. There are hundreds, if not thousands, of books on Buddhism that you could read, but few of them give the clarity of insight to be found in <u>Siddhartha</u>. Hesse is a writer of the first order and his simple, direct style brings home his points with extreme clarity.

We are all familiar with the orange chiffon robes of Buddhist monks. We have seen several recent movies and documentaries that have familiarized ourselves with these austere folks who like to live high in the mountains if at all possible. What we do not understand is why they live as they do. Let me tell the tale of the early days of the Buddha. The future Buddha is a prince among the people and lives a rollicking lifestyle full of the satisfaction of any and all physical desires. He marries and looks forward to the grand future his worldly position affords him. Sometime in early adulthood Buddha is overtaken by the need to seek enlightenment. He wanders through rivers, mountains, and lands starving toward knowledge. When the Buddha is all but dead from fasting he finds enlightenment under the Bodhi Tree.

Now a skeptic might point out that all that really happened is that Buddha has a delusional moment under the duress of hunger, but nevertheless the young prince becomes Guatama Buddha and starts not a religion, but a way of life. The eight-fold way to be exact. The foundation of Buddhism is the idea of endless reincarnation until one discovers and follows the path to enlightenment, which is the melding of your soul into the great soul, ending with nirvana. Until this happens you will be reborn endless times. What Buddha finds under the Bodhi tree is essentially the "middle way" the path between extreme indulgence and extreme deprivation. The Buddha would be punished in our society for abandoning his family, but in the east he is transformed into a great soul.

I could debate the pros and cons of east versus west, or enlightenment over salvation, but the truth is that no truth loving, soul searching individual can call his education complete who does not at least have a fundamental working knowledge of what Buddhism is all about. I contend that one can even be a Buddhist and a Christian simultaneously if one wishes. Remember the all-important truth that Buddhism is not a religion. Buddha founded it as a way to live ones life in order to achieve maximum results in this world and the next and does not preclude that a practitioner can hold other beliefs.

Hesse achieves a simplicity in his description of Buddhism and Siddhartha's life of searching that in my reading is unparalleled, even Jack Kerouac, a writer whose books I also recommend, stumbles over the details of Buddhist life. This stumbling by many authors is due to the attempt at over dramatization of what is fundamentally a simple man with a simple plan and a simple path of existence. Hesse captures this simplicity in a unique way through the telling of the life story of Siddhartha. Siddhartha is clumsy at first in his attempts at understanding, but through diligence and perseverance he is led to the path of enlightenment by the forces of nature. Siddhartha meets Buddha who is quickly gaining followers and practitioners. And over the hundreds of years since Buddha's death his followers have grown into the millions upon millions.

Hesse has written several other books written in the same simple style. But I recommend Siddhartha the most. It captures the sense of struggle both internal and external that Siddhartha must have experienced on his path. It is easy for westerners to pass off the ramblings of this seeking soul as little more than heathen babble. However, I can say with full understanding that Siddhartha is a book for the ages and has much to teach the westerner concerning how to live on an overcrowded, over polluted world without going stark raving mad. Read this short, involving book early on if not first and you will have an excellent gauge by which to judge the western books that follow.

WALDEN

This is another excellent book to start out with, primarily because it gives a firm moral compass to much that is to come. <u>Walden</u> by Henry David Thoreau is the story of the period of time Thoreau spent living in a small cabin on the edge of a pond in Massachusetts. I have been to Walden Pond and was amused to find it so near Boston and in the thick of one of most heavily populated regions of The United States. Walden Pond is hardly still the isolated outpost of the Thoreau years. But in the mid eighteen hundreds, the pond was still in a lazily inhabited area of New England and there were, at Thoreau's time, no other full time residents in the immediate area. However, even in Thoreau's time one could see the smoke from passing railroad engines riding the tracks to the west of the pond.

And just what did Henry do with all this free time he claimed for himself. Well, he watched a lot. He watched a battle between ants and the paths of waterfowl. He made the acquaintance of game and beasts, of fire and boat. Thoreau started by building a small cabin in the northwest corner of the lake. The cabin is no longer there, but the foundation is. The exact location of the cabin is known precisely and it sits back from the water much farther than I would have suspected from reading the book. However, I assure you this was indeed a primitive arrangement with only the barest of essentials for human life.

Thoreau keeps a diligent record of all his expenditures and the entire year comes to a grand total of three lattes. That's living cheap my friends. Henry's point is that all of us live more indulgently than we need to and economy of living leads to an abundance of thought. Henry is without a doubt one of the first environmentalists. This is his true crown in the world. Even in the sparsely populated times of the mid 1800's Henry understood that waste leads to disaster if allowed to be indulged on a grand enough scale. His deep insight into human nature allows him to contemplate the fatal flaw of democracy, the flaw is that if everyone is involved in his or her own struggle for wealth no one is looking out for the planet as a whole. The civilized society that is unconcerned for the need for conservation is doomed to follow the logical consequences of their folly to its ultimate doom.

I will mention here that <u>Walden</u> is not Thoreau's only work of literature. I will save you countless hours by forbidding you to even look up the titles to any other works by this man other than his brilliant little essay about "civil disobedience." The reason for this stricture is simple, Henry wrote a masterpiece, once. Unfortunately, he was never able to repeat this accomplishment. His other works are near drivel. It is hard to decide whether Henry was a brilliant writer who frittered away his talent after <u>Walden</u> or a mediocre writer who had lightening strike. I subscribe to the lightening interpretation, but that in no way hinders the sheer genius of Henry's little book about a pond.

What I admire the most about <u>Walden</u> is its sense that an entire community of beings lives in or near the water. Thoreau sees the ecosystem as a whole and not as a random group of individuals each struggling for their own existence. This is where the book achieves its power. This was an amazing leap of insight in its day. The symbiosis of nature was the focal point of Henry's life at the pond and the reason we love the book today. He showed that harmony of nature goes way beyond the bee's pollination of local flowers and to the fact that each cog in the mighty flow of the universe is inexorably connected to every other. Western man strives to isolate, to be a minimalist, yet nature becomes a contradiction at this level. Nature retreats under intense scrutiny into a self-defining loss of words. Henry's insight into the ecosystem around him has been a prime mover in the environmental movement of our time. This alone makes <u>Walden</u> worth the reading.

It must be noted that Thoreau did not live in complete isolation during his tenure at the pond. He had guests and the cabin was only an afternoon walk into the city of Concord. But the bulk of the story attends him in the private moments of reflection that are in our time a luxury of the highest order. We, the seekers after all things new and shiny, are encouraged by our society to "get busy", or as Eric Hoffer said, "We have been taught not to waste our time, but we have been taught to waste our lives." Read this glorious book and then tell me you see the world in the same old light of consumption.

THE BROTHERS
KARAMAZOV

Okay. You have had it easy up until now. Two good books to start that have only required a modest investment of time. Now we need to sink into the real meat of literature, the Russian novel. I'm not completely sure why the Russians are the greatest novelists of all time. Perhaps it is due to the extreme conditions in which they had to live combined with long lonely winter nights in which to indulge in the beauty of thousand page books. I'm not certain of the cause, but I am grateful for the effect. Fyodor Dostoyevsky wrote two of the four best novels ever written and both will be included in this book as recommended reading. This book is long, about 850 pages depending on what printing you read, so I encourage you to bite it off in small chunks. It is a savory meal I promise you.

Dostoyevsky was a very conflicted man who was prone to violent outbursts. By all accounts he treated everyone around him very badly. I say so what, what's a little spat between friends compared to millennium enduring masterpieces. Dostoyevsky wrote several other pieces more than worthy of your time "Notes From The Underground" among them, but I am focusing in this book on full-length works that give the general drift of an artist's entire life and times. Let it be said that you could do far worse than to read everything this man ever wrote. And why is he so worthwhile? I believe it is due to a keen perception combined with the harsh realities of both his inner and outer life mixed together with a fine economy of language. You rarely see Dostoyevsky quoted, but you hear him talked about always.

The Brothers Karamazov is epic in proportion, taking the intertwining lives of four brothers through a major portion of their adult lives. Each brother more or less represents an archetype, meaning the religious, the scholarly, etcetera. I don't want to dwell too much on the actual content of the book. The book more than speaks for itself. It is the enduring landscape of eighteenth century Russia that endows the work with life and substance. You have never understood true cold until you have read Dostoyevsky. The social conditions, the terrain, the weather, the blathering of inane Czars all give the Russia of his time a depth and reality that would be impossible to duplicate elsewhere. Russia is the only land to be born into if one aspires to be a novelist. It requires long pages of description to even touch on the grandeur and harshness of so great a land.

Dostoyevsky always gives the impression of a man who is living on borrowed time and doesn't give a damn what you or anyone else thinks. Here's why. In 1849, when he was still a young man, he was rounded up for political dissidence and hoisted across the frozen tundra to Siberia, there to be summarily shot. He is led out, attached to a pole I believe, and blindfolded. The order is given and the rifles raised. Dostoyevsky is prepared to die. Then another order, don't shoot. The whole execution is called off and Dostoyevsky, after serving a long and hard decade, is released back to the civilized world. Try that little experience and see if you don't come out of it with a chip on your shoulder.

In The Brothers Karamazov Dostoyevsky explores the purposes of society and the meaning of an individual existence in a world that is as cruel as it is absurd. He draws very few conclusions, his gift is to show the world as it is and let you decide for yourself what a stinking cesspool it is. If you are like me you will begin this book and be unable to put it down. Its insights into the human condition are unsurpassed in all of literature; by comparison Shakespeare is a mere tattler. I cannot even think of this book without the thought of bitter cold and starvation washing over me. This book is life altering, soak it in and revel in it. You will thank me.

Getting back to the book itself, I want to mention that within the book there is a chapter titled "The Grand Inquisitor" that is sometimes separated out and sold separately. If possible read this twice. Why? Because it is the greatest chapter of prose ever written. Though I rank War and Peace as the greatest novel of all time, The Brothers Karamazov a close second, I feel that this one chapter surpasses all that is in Tolstoy in sheer audacity, creativity and raw emotional power. The chapter concerns the second coming of Christ and the struggle of good and evil within each and every individual. I leave you with this challenge, jot down a few ideas in a journal about how you perceive the individual's journey through life and his struggle to ingrain sanity on the world and then write down your thoughts after reading this book. The thoughts will be miles apart, if not you need to read it again, you missed something important along the way.

THE REPUBLIC

Our reading skills should be at razor sharpness after our last outing into Russia, so this next assignment should be a breeze, but it's not. There is so much meat in <u>The Republic</u> that a slow burn of a read is called for. Plato is by most accounts the greatest philosopher who ever lived. Certainly he was the greatest philosopher of his age. Plato's ideas are still a part of our modern culture and he is assigned reading in every university in the west. What makes him so great? Well, for one, his introduction of the dialogue as a form of reasoning and argument. That's a nice start. Next, his overpowering dependence on ideas above that of the material world, and lastly, his use of the insufferable, yet loveable, character of Socrates from whom Plato learned a great deal of his early lessons.

It has been argued long and bitterly over where exactly Plato starts and Socrates ends. We would have no knowledge today of Socrates, save for a brief reference in the play "The Clouds" were it not for Plato. I believe it is generally agreed that most of the early works were written versions of Socrates' own teachings, but the rest of Plato is all his own. <u>The Republic</u> is most certainly the work of Plato alone. There is little hint of Socrates' own thoughts here. One can if one wishes obtain a book with all of Plato's works in one volume. I own one and it is 1186 pages long. However, as much as I love and admire Plato he gets a little redundant and tiresome in some of his lesser-known works. The essence of Plato is in <u>The Republic</u> and a man or woman can get the solid foundation of Greek philosophy from this book alone.

Just what is <u>The Republic</u>? Well, it is Plato's ideas on the perfect society and what constitutes justice and reality. In this book one will find two of the best-known ideas of western man. Both ideas are integral parts of our culture and thought to this day. One, of course, is the idea of a philosopher-king. Plato believed that a man of learning and wisdom should head society and down from him the rest of society should function much as an individual does with various parts and services performed by various classes of men. If this sounds like the caste system of India, that's because there are more than a few similarities. Much of the criticism of Plato's ideas focuses on just how one decides who performs what tasks and how one decides merit.

The other great idea is the concept of Plato's Cave. If you have never read Plato you have undoubtedly heard of this idea. Wouldn't it be wonderful to actually know what the hell people are talking about when they refer to it? Millions of people have used the allegory of the cave without the slightest clue as to what Plato meant by the example and how he meant for it to be understood. Basically, Plato believed that the reality that we see in our common everyday experience is an illusion. He taught that these images, which we believe are real, are actually like shadows cast upon a wall. He gives the example of people who are tied to a position inside a cave where they can only see the shadows that passing people and objects cast on a far wall. Their whole lives these people believe they are looking at the real world, yet all the time it is only a representation of reality. In Plato's world ideas are king. Each and every material thing in the world, according to Plato, is a form of the perfect idea of that thing in the world of ideas. Despite all the advances of science since Plato's time, no one has yet ruled out the possibility that all of reality is merely a grand idea made flesh.

Plato's other grand achievement is the establishment of "The Academy." Here Aristotle came to learn from the master. Aristotle, seeking his own place in the sun, came to disagree with Plato on many issues. Aristotle tried to describe nature in more scientific terms. However, as was the case in the Greek world, Aristotle did not perform many experiments to prove his theories, so today one is forced to laugh at many of Aristotle's notions. This is why I will not include any of the works of Aristotle in this book, but if you must read him I suggest the essay on drama as the most worthwhile.

Plato was born into a rank of privilege, yet lived a life dedicated to the understanding of the universe. To the extent he succeeded we still quote him today. In a recent war movie just released in 2002 his famous quote, "Only the dead have seen the end of war" was used in the opening scene. Plato is still a vibrant and vigorous read all these centuries later largely because he focused on ideas rather than mundane explanations. For all of the Greeks intellectual accomplishments most of their ideas concerning nature have been overturned by science, this due to their lack of experimentation, only Plato and mathematics remain. So it is fitting that <u>The Republic</u> take its place as the fundamental source of all political thought. It is one of the best books I have ever read or ever hope to read.

ON THE ROAD

It is time to leave the ancient world and enter the recently departed twentieth century. Few eras of American life interest me as much as the post World War II era that Jack Kerouac dubbed "the beat generation." I have read all but one of Kerouac's books and believe him to be one of the most engaged minds I have ever encountered. I love his writings, and though scholars haggle over the lasting value of his "spontaneous prose" I have already licked the platter clean and come back for seconds, and thirds. There is immediacy to his writing that is lost in the constant revision methods of normal literature. He is not so much writing as he is talking straight into your soul. Few authors have ever achieved such a glorious state.

Who was Jack Kerouac? He was an American born in Lowell, Massachusetts in the 1930's and came into adulthood in the late 1950's. He was a gifted athlete who excelled in football and the sprints and attended Columbia for one year before dropping out to explore the world. And what did he explore? Mostly America, via the long sleek ribbons of asphalt known as the American Highway System. After a stint in the Merchant Marines Kerouac fell in with a bunch of literary types who frequented such places as Greenwich Village. He was closely associated with Alan Ginsberg, Neil Cassidy and William Burroughs among others. His greatest literary achievement might perhaps be a little read book titled "Visions of Cody", but there is so much more to learn about America in <u>On The Road</u>.

After the war, Americans, to Kerouac, seemed "beat" meaning worn down, out on there luck, drifting. Kerouac, along with road sidekick Neil Cassidy, a womanizing child of a hobo, spent years of their early adulthood running back and forth between Denver, San Francisco, Lowell, and even Mexico. Though there are those who see this book as about the misguided ramblings of a bunch of losers, I assure you it is a book about the soul of America as sure as any ever written. What Kerouac sees in the America of the 1950's is a nation in search of meaning outside the venue of war. What the "beat generation" of literati was looking for specifically was a new form of expression modeled on the wonderful spontaneous quality of jazz.

Legend has it that <u>On The Road</u> was written on a single roll of paper and was carried by Kerouac in a valise for years. That sounds about par for Kerouac. Jack published one traditional novel at about the time he lived on the road. By traditional I mean he wrote it, rewrote it, and rewrote it again. According to Kerouac, <u>On The Road</u> was written exactly as you see it printed, although several contemporaries have alluded to the fact that they read various versions over the years. Nevertheless, Kerouac achieves a vision of America unlike any other and sets the stage for the "hippies" to come. The idea of restless energy spent roaming in search of meaning is really a "beat generation" ideal. And do not confuse the goateed, bongo banging poets of TV fame with the true "beats," the true "beats" were a beautiful and intellectually robust group. Their version of life as it should be lived has nothing to do with the bastardization of their ideals to be found in popular culture.

Kerouac states at the outset that he is always drawn to the "mad ones," those who are mad to live, mad to love, mad to travel. Kerouac finds the perfect muse in the disheveled life of one Neil Cassidy, one of the most famous figures of the sixties. Cassidy went on to further fame by being the driver of the "merry prankster" bus of author Ken Kesey. Cassidy was by many accounts a petty con man, but Kerouac sees in Neil a fallen angel, a saint of the road. As the book progresses the odd thing is that even the staunchest Cassidy haters come around to understanding that Kerouac is right. Cassidy exhibits the loose morals, no foundation school of life. Cassidy, during the course of the few years described in the book marries and divorces, marries, and has three or four kids in various locations around the country. So to me the scoundrel aspect of Cassidy's life is pretty well documented. But make no mistake; you are not likely to forget the driven and full throttle life of one Neil Cassidy. Neil was born to a hobo father and spent much of his childhood around Denver riding the rails. He spent time in reform schools, pool halls and whorehouses, but precious little in school.

If Kerouac is to be believed Neil Cassidy could have been one of the greatest writers of the twentieth century. The few letters and writing fragments Neil left behind suggest he would certainly have been the purest example of "spontaneous prose" of the era. Kerouac struggles mightily to duplicate the extemporaneous quality of Neil's letters, but ultimately fails even though Kerouac is a superior writer. Cassidy was too driven, too energetic, too "mad" to set down on paper the wild rush that was his life. Kerouac's book ultimately is about the rootlessness of America itself. Cassidy is merely the best example he has on hand. But Kerouac's love and admiration for "Dean Moriarity," as Cassidy is called in the book, shines through on every page. Kerouac was in love with the madness of the world and as the book ends and Kerouac has left the road and the frenetic comings and goings of his friend he sits and ponders what he has learned and what he has lost. Kerouac's famous ending "I think of Dean Moriarity, old Dean Moriarity, the father we never knew, I think of Dean Moriarity," rings in the ears of anyone who has touched this book and I too "think of Dean Moriarity" more than anyone might ever imagine.

LEAVES OF GRASS

I thought to leave poetry out of this book altogether. In reality there are very few "books" of poetry. Most poetry of note is to be found in collections gathered long after the artist's death. However, <u>Leaves Of Grass</u> is a notable exception, and so I wish to include this great book as part of any real self-education. Walt Whitman, by all accounts, was primarily himself a self-educated man. He dabbled in the newspaper business, was editor of one or two small publications, and wrote several essays that are now mostly ignored. For all his poetical genius Whitman wrote stunted prose that is difficult to read. But <u>Leaves Of Grass</u> is an absolute wonder to anyone who has never been blessed to read from its pages. Glistening with the solid musk of life, the thick mucous of death and the ripe fruit of love it is the greatest poetical work of all time. Shakespeare was a playwright, and the greatest one at that, but folks, he was not a poet. Walt Whitman is a poet, and one of the few human beings who are genuinely worthy of that name.

While many poets take as their canvas the countryside, failed love relationships or even battle, Whitman takes the entire universe as his. And not just the present or near future, but all of history and all of the future, to the end of time. Whitman's greatness is to be found in this exalted state of all encompassing thought. Whitman looks to the past and finds the seeds of America, he looks to the future, and he sees the vast communication networks that are soon to be. He looks into the very body of man and sees the electrical impulses swirling in the veins. He sees love as not just the magical manifestation of romance, but as a flesh and blood reality born of hormones and need. He sees grass as the "fresh uncut hair of graves."

Walt Whitman was also a man of his times and those times included the Civil War. He volunteered in the medical tents to give water to the wounded, to clean dressings and to take down letters back home. Cries of "Walt, Walt" could be heard throughout the tents of the wounded. He passed daily the stacks of arms and legs that had been amputated the night before by surgeons. Some of Walt's greatest poetry is included in the section "Drum Taps" that sets down his feelings and experiences during the war. A contemporary of Abraham Lincoln, Whitman writes two of the best poems about Lincoln's loss ever written. While you may be familiar with the rare rhyming quality of "Captain, My Captain" written in rhyme to be read by the masses, the better poem is "When Lilacs Last In The Dooryard Bloomed" arguably the best poem ever written.

Walt Whitman as a person is a bit of an enigma. He never married, was presumed homosexual, although many debate that he was sexual in any true sense of the word, and wandered the wilderness and roads of Manhattan and New Jersey. He worked day jobs, odd jobs, and occasionally a real job in the newspapers, but generally spent the vast majority of his life unattached to the material qualities of life. He did travel to Europe in his old age and to New Orleans in his prime, but spent the vast majority of his life within a hundred miles of where it began. His family, especially his mother, was emotionally stifling and this fact is said to have had a profound effect on Whitman's ability to deal with the everyday world. However, I slightly disagree, genius is a lonely business, quoting myself in one of my own books "the burden of genius is to have no peers." And Walt Whitman was a genius if ever I have encountered one.

You may need to reread some of the poems in Leaves Of Grass, this is totally understandable and expected. I have read the book four times at least. The meat of many of Whitman's poems only comes out after the passages have become somewhat familiar. But be prepared also for the disjointed quality of his passages. These are not simple rhymes. These poems bristle with life and intelligence and challenge the mind to think in new ways. When one encounters Whitman one encounters a great soul. His intelligence is as deep as the ocean and his interest as long as time and his words are as profound as any ever written and have only grown more prophetic with the passing years. Leaves Of Grass was no instant hit or bestseller. It has taken a century for America to come to terms with its poetical mystic. But as in many cases, Europe discovered Walt first and sent word back across the sea. Drink in this delicious nectar of words and I guarantee you will be profoundly changed by the experience.

THE BIBLE

What, you say? The Bible to be read as self-educating literature? You bet. We can debate the revelatory nature of the Old and New Testament until the end of time, but the obvious truth is that the Bible contains some of the greatest stories, poems, proverbs, and history of any book ever written. No person should be unfamiliar with its pages. How many times in your life have you heard people quote the Bible but later admit to you that they never actually read the thing. That is disgraceful, every thinking, feeling, rational being must be required to read this marvelous work of literature and I don't care if you are Muslim, Buddhist or Hindu, my point here is not an evaluation of the book as divine truth, but its literary qualities. This book is a must read for anyone who can even remotely qualify as an educated person. So many of our culture's sayings, laws, modes of conduct and beliefs can be traced back to the Bible. You must know the source of the river to get a true idea of where the river is going.

I recommend that you read the Bible in the order it is presented in most editions. There is a history flowing forward here of a people that still exist. To skip around is to lose the fundamental structure of that history and to lose the profound examples told along the way. I do not believe that the entire Bible is an exact account of the Hebrew people. Some of it rings true, such as Deuteronomy, but other sections do not, such as Job and the tale of Sampson. These read more like allegories and very fine ones at that. But don't think I am stepping on your religious toes here. I am only making a personal observation. You may believe what you wish to believe.

The Bible starts with an account of creation. This account bears little resemblance to the "Big Bang" theory, as we are currently familiar with it. In Genesis, God and God alone creates the world out of a void and God breaths form and life into the world by his power. God lights the heavens and the night, places animals and man in Eden, and generally gets the ball rolling. The story of the Garden of Eden, in which man is responsible for his own fall, is the Bible's way of dealing with the age old question of how does a just and perfect God create evil. The answer here is, He didn't, He only allowed evil to test men for their worthiness to enter into an eternal rest with Him in heaven. Now the problem here is that most men have lived and died on this planet without ever having even heard of the Hebrew God and most who have heard of Him do not follow His teachings, therefore if one is to follow the logic through, God created man to live with Him in heaven although a very high percentage will instead dwell for eternity in hell. Something is amiss here.

Nearly every culture, from the aborigines of Australia to the Eskimos of Alaska, possesses a creation myth to explain the world. Most of these were created long before science came long and disputed some of the findings so you must bear with the flaws in the Bible to get at the heart of the matter, which is how to take a group of slaves and transform them into enlightened beings capable of high civilization, high religious understanding and worldly might and wealth. Folks, this is an allegory for the whole rise of mankind since the dawn of Homo Sapiens. And as such it is an invaluable tool. The various failings of individuals such as Sampson and David are examples of societies at large who rise and then fall because of their own misdeeds and arrogance. Job is a lesson in patience with the role of evolution in creating truly perfect and happy human beings, it is a wake up call to our minds that we humans are not a finished product, we are only capable of being perfected at some distant time in the future.

The writings of the Old Testament prophets are of great value, but are highly uneven. We tread between the extremes of Isaiah, a literary master, and minor prophets such as Joel who probably could have been left out of the book altogether. In between we have two examples of great literature that must be read with care. The Psalms of David and Ecclesiastes, said to be the work of Solomon. These two sections are full of great words and even greater thoughts. I believe that these two individuals are real characters of history, these two sections are not idealized or patronized works scribbled by scribes and attributed to kings, they are real literary works direct from the human heart and are priceless gifts to the world.

Let's move on to the New Testament. I believe absolutely that Jesus of Nazareth was a true flesh and blood human being. There is enough evidence to convict him of actually having walked the shores of Galilee. Was he the Son of God? Unanswerable, so lets move past that into what we do know and that is that the man taught beautiful things to simple people. Sometimes in our more enlightened age we lose the simplicity of human conduct in a vast array of murky shades of gray. Is withholding information lying, we ask? Is a president exempt from the law? Are all things moral, relative? But in that simple pastoral world of Jesus it was your heart, your intentions, that saved or condemned you. How simple, yet effective.

The world of Palestine in the time of Jesus was a world dominated by Roman occupation. As such the rule of force was everywhere and seen as the surest sign of Roman inferiority. Romans were simple barbarians who, though skilled in war and architecture, failed in the estimation of the Jews to evolve to a high civilization. The reason was the Roman's insistence on rule by force. Jesus, and I should say a great many others as well, grew up in this world loathing all things pertaining to physical power. These mystics and prophets, teachers and lecturers strove to rid the Romans of their power by igniting a deeper power within the human heart. In other words to deny that the Roman power had any lasting effect compared with the eternal life promised by Jesus.

Though Jesus was eventually crucified for defying Roman power his words were so powerful that four hundred or so years later they were adopted by the Roman Empire. Jesus taught such masterpieces of thought such as "love thy neighbor as thyself," "seek ye first the kingdom of heaven and all things shall be added unto you." Brilliant religious thought and that is why the religion founded by Jesus has endured. It fulfills a need by the common people to be assured that his or her sufferings and sacrifices are not in vain. Jesus promised that if they endured well, they would live with him forever in heaven. Such promises are hard to ignore. Nevertheless Jesus was a great teacher whose simple metaphors and bold statements ring through the centuries along with the words of Paul who wrote many of the best books of the New Testament. Read and be changed.

CRIME AND PUNISHMENT

We return again to the luxurious pastures of Dostoyevsky. I assure you it is a rich milk and ale we imbibe herein. <u>Crime and Punishment</u> is one of the four greatest novels ever written. It is compelling even in our own time for its clear examination of the criminal mind. Roskolnikov, the main character and murderer, is haunted throughout by the guilt that resonates from his own thoughts. He convicts himself, in other words. Eventually, Roskolnikov is hounded by a detective and driven mad by his own torment. This rings very true for a man with a conscious. We somehow accept that he will be weighed down by the heft of his guilt. But in our day and age we see so many criminals who exhibit no remorse whatsoever. This is the dividing line between the centuries. Whereas a resident of the nineteenth century says, "How can he live with himself," many in our day say, "Why didn't he do a better job of covering it up?"

It is in the difference in the interpretation of guilt that much can be learned about the two disparate centuries. And, I might add, how we have gone from a culture of control by guilt to a culture of control by force and law. Roskolnikov seems out of place in our century like a country hick who just jumps off the turnip truck and immediately assumes everyone he meets will be as honest as he himself is honest. I found Roskolnikov a strange being, a man who suffers his guilt and allows the guilt to dissolve his sanity. This seems so odd in our "get away with it mentality." It seems to modern men that Roskolnikov's true problem is that he is weak. But in truth he has taken action against corruption, which he sees as bleeding the people of their right to eat. It is the second murder that he commits, to cover up the first, wherein Roskolnikov becomes the eternal criminal.

However, it is the beautiful way in which Dostoyevsky brings about Roskolnikov's own downfall that is the true power of the novel. I doubt if any book ever written has so captured the nature of our own thoughts. You feel as you read this book that you are for a time living in Roskolnikov's own head. This book, as well, has some of the most vivid descriptions of Russia's damnable weather and perhaps the best descriptions of cold weather ever written. I felt for a time the shivering cold, the blistering wind and the depths of struggle that simply living in so harsh an environment produces. After Dostoyevsky I felt I had actually been to Russia. That is a high compliment for a writer to receive. And Dostoyevsky is the greatest novelist that has ever lived. I say that despite the fact that I will present in this book <u>War and Peace</u> as the greatest novel ever written. These are two separate facts.

Dostoyevsky is not a prim and proper writer writing in the sparse vacuum of a serene and contemplative life. He is a man who has lived, suffered, struggled, ached, and endured and all these attributes come gushing forth in his greatest works. Dostoyevsky wrote four novels that are considered masterpieces and two shorter works that are masterworks as well ("Notes From the Underground" and "The Dream of a Ridiculous Man") and if you ever get the time they are more than worthwhile. However, the big two as I call them, <u>The Brothers Karamozov</u> and <u>Crime and Punishment</u> will suffice for this book. When I first discovered Dostoyevsky, and the Russian novel in general, I felt that I had discovered a path to Everest, and I had, the most difficult one. But make no mistake, reading the great Russian novelists is the most rewarding reading of all.

As I have said before I am not really sure what has produced this embarrassment of literary wealth, but I am sure the harshness of Russia's environment played more than a small part in it. In fact, the Russian novels that will be included in this book could almost form a subset of the few books that one must read to be considered literate. But I caution the reader here not to give full sway to the powerful lull of the Russian artist. It is possible to become completely absorbed in their world and forget that much remains to be discovered. I spent nearly a year of my life knee deep in Russian novels and almost did not emerge on the other side where a man still possesses the vague hope of a better world. So use caution and enjoy, <u>Crime and Punishment</u> is a feast of the human imagination.

THE CATCHER IN THE RYE

It is impossible to say exactly why J. D. Salinger hit the nail on the head of juvenile angst in this wonderful book about alienation, but I suspect that more than a few adults have seen themselves in the character of Holden Caulfield. The book rings as true for the forty-year-old going through a midlife crisis as it does for the fifteen-year-old struggling with the difficulties of puberty. What struck me most in reading this book was the callous way in which Holden treats the world, but then, he feels apart from it. The institution that is the boarding school is a wonderful metaphor for the adult trappings of corporations and clubs. Holden Caulfield is everyman as he walks bitterly and cautiously through the minefield of the world. Adults love the book as much as the young do.

I profess to know little of Salinger's life other than that he lives on a farm somewhere in the east and that Joyce Maynard visited him and fell in love with him when she was eighteen. His daughter has also written a scathing expose on his failings as a father. But this lack of information is to be excused because the man is a recluse of the first order. He is said to be so sensitive to criticism that he has saved all of his subsequent writings for publication after his death. I have a gut feeling that we are to be gravely disappointed by these works when we see them, expecting each of them to surpass <u>The Catcher In The Rye</u>. None of them will. Salinger is not a great writer in the traditional sense, he is not a Hemingway or a Fitzgerald or even a Steinbeck. Salinger is a writer of the second rank who fell magically into a pasture and came out smelling like fresh daisies. In other words <u>The Catcher In The Rye</u> is a bit of serendipity that fell into the world through a writer that had little idea that he was writing the definitive work on juvenile angst. The book is a happy accident that we can be grateful for, but rest assured there are no other such works hovering in Salinger's briefcase. He struck lightening once and I believe his grave reluctance to publish now is in fact a full understanding by Mr. Salinger that he has already disseminated his best work. I would love to be proven wrong, unfortunately, when it comes to books, I rarely am.

Through the eyes of Holden Caulfield (by the way this book still sells something like 500,000 copies a year worldwide) we see the result of society's compartmentalizing of the human spirit. Holden is put into a boarding school to be warehoused until ready for shipping out into the world. However, he is also learning that he cares as little for the world as the world cares for him. Holden's parents are emotionally missing from the book. I do not know to what extent this book is based on Salinger's own predilection toward isolation, but I suspect it is quite ably a true record of his own feelings concerning the world. This is why the book resonates so well with older readers. I did not read the book until I was about 32 and had four children, yet I still found the book compelling and true in my own life. This is the main reason for its continued popularity. It is a book about the way everybody feels about the world internally, but these feelings are rarely expressed vocally because adults are supposed to have a handle on the world.

The other magical property of the book is that it is set in a time that is every time. Meaning that the book does not necessarily betray a specific time and place. Therefore it is easy for every new rising generation to think they are reinventing teen angst and having that angst revealed in this book. Truthfully, if I were to write a best selling book I would definitely want this quality to appear. This book will be as fresh and vital a hundred years from now as it is today and as it was twenty years ago. It is like Hamlet in that way. Hamlet rings true centuries later because the struggle of Hamlet is every man's struggle. So too is Holden Caulfield's struggle the struggle of every human being to find purpose and meaning in an increasingly isolating world. I suspect that my great grandchildren will read <u>The Catcher In The Rye</u> one day and think it is a new book just released. That is a great thing to say about a book.

THE GRAPES OF WRATH

There are actually nitwits who argue over whether John Steinbeck was a great writer or not. <u>The Grapes of Wrath</u> dispels this idea for all of time. Steinbeck's shortcoming as a writer was that he published books that shouldn't have been published. In other words, he wrote a couple a three real stinkers, but he also wrote a couple a three real masterpieces. I choose here to forgive John his failures because I am first and foremost a true believer in failure; failure is often just a bump on the road to ultimate success. So lets proceed even though I will admit up front that not every word John Steinbeck wrote is the "word of God."

<u>The Grapes Of Wrath</u>, for the three of you who have not seen the movie, is the story of the Joad family as they migrate from the dust-bowl of Oklahoma to what they hope is a great new life of endless work in California. However, when they arrive they are about as welcome as a group of travelers carrying the Bubonic Plague. They quickly realize the offers of work were all a great hoax and they continue their sufferings into northern California where they do at least find enough work to subsist. The journey the Joads make along

Route 66 is legendary as a prototype of countless thousands of similar journeys made by real people during the dustbowl years. I have commented in one of my books that the Joads were much better off than my own predecessors who didn't even have a hood on their jalopy.

That the book is all a thin mask for a communistic agenda is all bunk. It was only a thinly veiled attempt by Steinbeck to find a way for people to eat. It must be remembered that at the time it was no certain bet as to whether communism or capitalism was the best way to feed people. The Communist party in the dust bowl years was a viable alternative. However, the truth of the great depression was that capitalism was indeed the better system so long as it had some help from the government, particularly this was true of banks who needed the support of the federal government to prevent runs on their reserves. In the end the dustbowl migration sent a lot of needed people to California and Oregon. It balanced the country east and west. My own family ended up in the Willamette Valley of Oregon due to the migration and forty-five years later produced its first college graduate-me.

But if you have only seen the movie let me assure you that you have seen only the limited scope of Hollywood and not the complete treatment given the subject in the book. Steinbeck is filled with indignation at what these people were forced to suffer and had a big hand in helping to sway the government from its complacency into helping these folks out of their misery. Many children of these migratory folks have gone on to assume positions of responsibility and leadership in this country. We are all only a few steps from being on the down and out. Let us never forget that when we see the less fortunate. Steinbeck makes sure we never will.

I find gentleness in Steinbeck's writing that is unique. He cares about his subjects more than the average writer and he chooses most of his heroes and main characters from the downtrodden. Therefore they will always be more compelling than the tyrants and kings of Shakespeare. Steinbeck's world is peopled with simplicity and honesty and forthrightness that is lacking in the cultured and the privileged. I saw more humanity in the tragic figure of Lenny than in the Gatsby given us by Fitzgerald. I believe <u>The Grapes Of Wrath</u> to be one of the most important books ever written. Surely few books have had a greater impact on the society of their own times than this book. Steinbeck brought the cruelty and the shame of the situation to light in such a way that no moral people could ignore his message. Those of us who are the descendants of the "oakies" have a debt of gratitude to pay to John Steinbeck. I am right here paying mine by recommending his glorious book.

I want to make a final comment on the book itself. The ending in the book is ten times more powerful than the mush ending of the movie. Hollywood sidestepped the issue by eliminating the brilliant ending altogether. In the end of the book the Joads daughter feeds a dying, hungry man with milk from her own breast. It is one of the most powerful endings to a book I have ever read and I dare you to forget it anytime soon. And lastly, I have been to the Salinas area where Steinbeck lived. It is a rich and beautiful area filled with agriculture and sunshine. If I could have been born anywhere else on earth it would have been there, where I too would have grown up wondering how so much suffering can exist in so beautiful a world.

THE SUN ALSO RISES

Ah, we come to the world of Earnest Hemingway. Hemmingway is one of the most enduring figures of literature because his personal life became almost as large as his literary life. Hemmingway was born in Oak Park, Illinois and chased two world wars and Africa to boot during his tempestuous, yet fulfilled life. Earnest married four times, had three sons, lived in Paris, Key west, Cuba and finally, and fatally, Sun Valley, Idaho. His life is as legendary as his words, but make no mistake, the simple, direct and forthright style of Hemmingway is powerful and eternal. Although a person could do worse than reading all of Hemmingway's books I will recommend only two of his works in this book. The first, <u>The Sun Also Rises</u> was earnest's first full-length published work written when he was young man living in Paris. The book details the drunken revelry of a group of ex-patriots living in post war Paris that was later dubbed by Gertrude Stein as "The Lost Generation."

Hemmingway's compatriots during his Paris years included such literary notables as Don Dos Passos and F. Scott Fitzgerald. Earnest admired Fitzgerald greatly but thought him too frail for this world. Somehow Earnest is able to convince this group of ex-patriots to follow him to Pamplona to see the chasing of the bulls. Hemmingway

fell in love with bull fighting during his time in Spain and considered it the manliest of sports as well as the only place a writer could
contemplate death between wars. The group is a disparate bunch
who soon devolve into petty infighting and jealousy, as well as more
than a little of the "recipe." However, in this work Hemmingway is
able to capture a moment in time better than any of his contemporaries and his vivid dialogue breathes life back into the dried bones
of the "lost generation" and allows the modern reader to get
involved in that era more so than any history book ever could.

Hemmingway was a complex man, a man given to extremes of
masculinity and adventure. He loved the outdoors, especially hunting and fishing, and spent as much time as possible on his boat "The
Pilar." It has been suggested that Earnest adopted his manly persona
to cover up a queenly disposition. I think it must be said that this is
true. Hemmingway's son Gregory came out as a cross-dresser
shortly before his death. It ran in the family and the suffocation of
these feelings probably had a lot to do with all that depression the
Hemmingway family suffered through the years. Nevertheless, the
words remain and they are great words, clipped and polished to
razor fineness, spare and absolute in their telling and bold and reckless in their power. To read Hemmingway is to experience the actual
life of the story. He strove all his life to write "one true sentence"
and it is certain he wrote a thousand true sentences, if not more. His
books resonate with the vibrancy of some of the most tumultuous
times man has ever known and Hemmingway was always compelled
to be on the scene when war or adventure broke out.

Ultimately, despite all of his worldly success Hemmingway loses
his home in Cuba after Castro comes to power and Earnest flees to
Sun Valley, Idaho, where driven to severe depression, caused in part

by a head injury suffered while struggling to get out of a burning plane, he loads his shotgun for the last time and blows his brains out. I traveled not long ago to Sun Valley to get a sense of why Hemmingway loved this area. Sun Valley is a mountainous, vibrant land, with abundant hunting and skiing. Unfortunately, the Hemmingway home is owned by a society of some sort and not on public display. I would have loved to go inside and see how he lived. However, you can go to Key West, Florida and visit the house he lived in there, it is now a museum. For some reason it is impossible for me to only recommend you read Hemmingway's books. It seems necessary somehow that you delve at least a little into his vast life. Hemmingway was both writer and adventurer; the two cannot be separated without losing a sense of the man himself. Read <u>The Sun Also Rises</u> and develop a sense of the man who wrote it. You will be enriched beyond anything you have imagined.

MOBY DICK

Any list of the five greatest novels ever written must include <u>Moby Dick.</u> Although I place it in the number five position some may rate it higher. It must be remembered that this book was ignored upon publication and a financial disaster for its author. The book was considered too bogged down in the details of the whaler's life. Fortunately, Herman Melville did not change his book to please the paltry needs of the masses. What Melville has left us is a masterpiece of English literature and a chronicle of a time long past and forgotten. Thanks to Melville we will never be able to forget the whaling era of our New England past.

<u>Moby Dick</u> introduces us to two of the greatest characters in all of fiction. One, Captain Ahab, and two, Moby Dick, the whale. It is impossible to read this book and not find yourself months later struggling to figure out if the whale is chasing the man or the man chasing the whale. Doctoral theses have been written on the subject and no conclusion has ever been reached. In fact, that is the very definition of a great story, one that cannot be resolved with definite certainty. I suspect that in the year 3000 men will still be reading this book with the same wonder and amazement we read it today. Is the whale nature or God; is Ahab all men or just evil men? We will

never know because Melville himself did not know. Melville actually believed it was a story about a whale and a man, how naïve, we laugh.

I must caution the reader that it is very possible and perhaps even likely that you will find yourself so absorbed in this book that chores and commitments, work and school may fall by the wayside as you delve into a world that is both fascinating and absorbing. Yes there is a great deal of detail concerning whaling that might be skipped, but don't. That detail is as necessary as the sun is to life on earth. We must know the ropes, so to speak, before embarking on such a long and perilous voyage. The details are like a training class that prepares us for the gusts and gales to come. If ever there was written a book that should never have been made into a movie this is it. The full power and glory of <u>Moby Dick</u> is squashed under the incessant need to squeeze and compact story in to the available time. Skip the movie and read this book, I promise you it is worth every moment spent.

After a great deal of fiddling around the New England area we set to sea and soon captain Ahab is hell bent on finding a white whale that took his leg years before. The chase begins. Though it appears throughout the book that poor Moby Dick is doomed, ultimately, the big fish rams the ship and sinks it. Sweet revenge it would seem for all the trouble we caused little Moby, but after some five or six hundred pages you will be hard pressed to know just exactly what happened. Did the villain win? Did the evil captain Ahab get his just desserts? Was captain Ahab indeed evil? Was the innocent white whale really innocent? I'm still struggling with all these issues fifteen years after having read this book. In short I must conclude that <u>Moby Dick</u> is the perfect metaphor for the struggle of man against nature and the answer to many of these questions is simply a matter of which side you are on at the time. Moby Dick, the whale, is not God, I'm convinced of this, he represents nature and the pull of nature to eternally send men back to the caves they came out of. Ahab is not evil, in my opinion, he is obsessed, and the book can be read as a nice little treatise on obsession by any card carrying Freudian. This is master storytelling of the highest order and I would kill to think up such a glorious and rich adventure.

Melville suffered great ridicule during his life for his dull, long and misbegotten book. Let this be a lesson to any aspiring writer. If you write a good story it will find its way and endure long after the critics have been planted in shallow graves. The truly great and the truthful will endure beyond all attempts of the mediocre to stop them. This book has endured, will endure because it is a tireless theme that will never be resolved. In short, there is no answer to the questions raised in this book, it is all a matter of conscious, opinion and perspective, and indeed that may be, in time, the answer to the riddle of the universe itself.

THE WISDOM OF INSECURITY

This is a little known book by a little known writer named Alan Watts. Alan attempts in his books, of which there are many, to combine the teachings of the east and west into a coherent whole. He is the best writer of this genre I have ever encountered. His short, but powerful, masterpiece <u>The Wisdom Of Insecurity</u> is a must read for any thinking, reasoning being. The book presents issues and ideas that have resonated in my mind for twenty years and have grown and developed there until I believe many of Alan Watts's ideas to be genuine pieces of philosophical scripture. The question we must ask here is this-is there indeed wisdom in insecurity? Yes there is, if you follow his thinking full course that is, and not take the short cut of simply following the title to its easy to realize conclusion.

The thesis of this book is extremely difficult for the women I have explained it to understand. Women in most societies have been taught the exact opposite of Watt's teachings and indeed are perhaps protected by nature, as regards the rearing of young, to seek out security in anal retentive ways that astound men. As men in western culture we are allowed a certain risk taking mentality, up to a point.

Once a wife has been selected, children incubated and a house purchased we are supposed to give up our cavorting ways and "settle down." But is this course of action actually the wisest course for ones life? The answer is-sometimes, sometimes not.

The general principle of this book is a little more complicated than the title would suggest. What Alan Watts is saying is that men should not seek security for security's sake. To do this leads not only to constipated thinking, but also to a lack of material and spiritual growth in human beings. We are moved forward as a people by taking risks, by thinking new thoughts, by living daring, and perhaps, reckless lives. Although it is comfortable in our recliner, remote control in hand, these types of men did not conquer Everest. The risk takers determine progress, and wisdom and insight comes to those who can hold opposite thoughts in their heads and still live productive lives. When a man or woman takes as their primary goal in life the accumulation of security a certain rot cankers on the edges of their lives and they are lead to the grave in rapid, and unending, succession.

Alan brings into his book a great deal of the flavor of eastern thought and I contend that for any one who wants to understand his culture it is necessary to see it from an opposing point of view. In the east philosophy is more concerned with a holistic interpretation. We in the west have been trained to take things apart, to dissect, to minimilize, to scrutinize. In the east it is all one great body, this universe, and a man can no more tear apart a piece of a whole than he can remove his heart and still call himself alive. This fundamental difference in our understanding of the universe has led to many different opinions on the nature of art, business, architecture, and society. We see today many of the ideals of the east creeping into our western society. But we seek to meld these ideas into our current landscape of ideas. This is essentially what Watt's was attempting thirty years ago, before it was popular to do so. I believe that both east and west will benefit from our continued intercourse. Both disciplines have much to teach the other.

However, it is in the field of security, or rather the lack of security that Watt's hits the golden nail. I have thought long and hard about Watt's ideas concerning security. Sometimes I have vacillated as to which side of the issue I decided I was on, but through the years as more and more understanding floods into me I have concluded that security is not only the cancer of the soul, but the literal cause of many cancers. Think about the lifestyle of those who place security at the forefront of their lives. These folks come home to safe houses; eat food that has been processed and degermed. They sit in soft chairs and watch entertainment programs that mildly sedate them until it is time to go to bed and get eight unsettled hours of sleep worrying about the job. This is not living, is it? When one eschews security in favor of a life of exploration both mental and physical, life becomes a grand adventure of living for the day and not for the day we retire. Wealth comes to those who risk what they have to get more, love comes to those who risk rejection, life happens to those who chase it and occasionally catch it. Life does not seep into your family room, caress the Barcalounger and swirl you off your butt to action. Life is a dragon that must be chased and ridden, never subdued. Here's to insecurity, the wisest life I know.

TROPIC OF CANCER-TROPIC OF CAPRICORN

We come now to the world of Henry Miller. Miller was a man after my own heart. He believed most all work to be futile and in vain. Henry ran off to Paris to write, to be, I suppose, like the lost generation, but what he found in Paris was a perfectly good excuse to stay drunk and cavort in bars. I love Henry Miller both as a person and as a writer. Despite all the sexual bombast he was actually a very gentle and thoughtful man. His portrayal of women has gotten him into hot water in modern times, but these words wherein he allegedly degrades women were never written seriously. He was writing about himself, but as a character. The real Henry Miller was too shy and demure to have carried out a tenth of what is portrayed in his books.

The world of Henry Miller is peopled with layabouts, drunks, whores, and bums. It seems that writers are always attracted to the downtrodden. But Henry writes about this world with such true love and devotion that you get swept away by the power of this world. Henry spends most of his Paris days looking for work, looking for booze and looking for women. Not a bad life if you can find a way to eat. Success comes slowly for Henry, his books were too sexual for their times and were banned in many places. They still are, but the two masterpieces of Miller's life <u>The Tropic of Cancer</u> and <u>The Tropic of Capricorn</u> make up a volume of pure literature that is to be savored as an epic of the twentieth century. For the purposes of this book I am treating the two works as one for they are, in any real sense, part one and two of one colossal text. Henry eventually made his way to Big Sur and tried to create a colony of writers and artists and indeed an artistic movement, but this experiment was mostly a flop.

Why I include these two books in this work is harder to say, especially when one considers such books as <u>The Iliad</u> and <u>Plutarch's Lives</u> that will not be included. But you must remember the purpose of this book is to gain a self-education. Henry Miller will teach you more about the true world and about the ruin that too much hard work will bring than a hundred books on the subject written by well meaning, but ill-prepared professors. I feel like I've roamed the back alleys and the flophouses when I read Miller. He captures the flavor and the textures of the city that even Hemingway cannot surpass. And I might add that this book is as much about America as it is about Paris. All of the expatriates that formed the "lost generation," of which Miller was not included, said that they only understood America by leaving it. Miller, too, comes to his conclusions based on his departure and life abroad.

Why read Miller? Because there is nothing on earth like a good rollicking read and Miller is definitely that. His books bristle with intelligence and more than a little self-delusion. They are works that will stand the test of time and Henry Miller will in the future be considered one of the greatest writers of the twentieth century. True souls are hard to find and none were truer than Henry Miller. His writing is at times bombastic and his language can be said to be of a dialect no longer spoken-literate. Even I, whose vocabulary is considered large, always had to have a good dictionary on hand when I read Miller. I always suspected that Henry had one near by as well. So when Henry wanted to tease us into believing him he would open up the accursed book of words and find a word no one had ever heard of. Unfortunately, along with the strong sexual sense, the voluminous vocabulary of Miller gets in the way of the writing and left him a smaller audience than would have been the case. I often found it a better read to simply bypass those words and to just get lost in the moment of a Paris evening.

When one reads Henry Miller at his best (and to tell the truth he wrote one or two clunkers and repeated himself with his Nexus, Sexus, Plexus trilogy) the pure writing seeps into you and you find that you suddenly know more about the world than it was possible before. Miller opens the world like a chestnut and pours out the contents to be examined, and if unnecessary, discarded. I believe Miller to have been a great soul, a gentle soul, who truly wanted to teach man about himself. I would love to have cavorted with Miller in Paris, heck, kick in Hemingway and Kerouac and we just might have found the makings of a memorable night.

BIG SUR

Sometimes I have a special feeling for a book that is often ignored by the world. This is one of them. You may actually have a little trouble finding Big Sur in your local bookstore. I suggest a good used bookstore, or of course, ordering it online. There is a purpose to my madness in suggesting this book however. In On The Road we see the youthful exuberance of madness, the hunger, the passion, the drive to explore, to know, to get at life. What we see in Big Sur is the aftermath of this indulgence and as a denouement to youth it is unparalleled in its wisdom. You cannot read this wonder of a book without the whole weight of generational sadness washing over you. The "Beats" had become the "Drunks." Kerouac had come to the conclusion that all he had believed and written was just a poor highway to oblivion. The folly of youth is never on better display than in this work.

Big Sur is hardly Kerouac's best or second best book, that is not why I ask you to read it. Read it because it is revelatorier of human nature than a hundred better-written tomes. This is the old Kerouac, the Kerouac that has become disgusted with Neil Cassidy and with the depths of alcoholism and what drink has done to punish his life and that of his generation. This book is a lamentation. Written against the backdrop of Big Sur, a narrow strip of redwoods growing along a creek in northern California, the stark beauty of the landscape acts as contrast to the dark barren wasteland of Kerouac's own inner world. What better way is there to examine the meaning of life than to see the potential of life followed so vividly by the reality of all that has transpired, the end result of all the glorious possibilities with which we endowed our youth. Kerouac would live only a few more years after writing this book, done in by the bottle at 47.

Neil Cassidy, whom Kerouac made famous, went on to additional fame by being the main driver of the bus "Further" whose run across America was immortalized in the book The Electric Kool-Aid Acid Test. Cassidy died young as well. It seems that those who are "mad to live" are also first to die. Big Sur is the saddest book I know. I loved to read about Kerouac's adventures on the road or mountain climbing or even about his summer spent manning a lookout in Washington. And when you are so enthralled with Kerouac's world and wishing to pattern you own life on his example it is disparaging to come to a work so full of the bitterness and anger at having squandered much of your life in utter foolishness. When we are young the world is everything, when we are old the world is nothing. In between we find ourselves or lose ourselves forever.

THE TRUE BELIEVER

If you had difficulty finding my last selection get ready for a real test of your determination to complete this self-education project. <u>The True Believer</u> by Eric Hoffer, despite selling a half million copies in its day, is difficult to find. I live in a suburb of Portland, Oregon, arguably the book reading capital of the world and home to one of the largest used bookstores on earth, and I found and purchased one of only three copies I could find in the entire state. However, do not dismay, you can find this book with some effort, but you may have to check it out of the library. If this book were not worth the effort I wouldn't be suggesting you make it. This book is short and easy to read, but make no mistake; it is full of wisdom and enlightenment.

Eric Hoffer is a bit of an enigma. He worked for years as a migratory worker before landing on the docks for the remainder of his working life as a longshoreman. He worked on the docks right up to the day he retired despite the fact that he had published, successfully, several books. <u>The True Believer</u> is one of those rare finds. After a lifetime of reading what I thought was every worthy book, I did not discover this little masterpiece until I was 46 years old. And what a joy it was to read. Eric Hoffer strips his writing bare of pretense, haughty learning, redundancy and puffery. What we get for our money is a book that spells out in alarmingly clear prose the methods by which mass movements are orchestrated by both the evil and the wise. Written shortly after the end of World War II the book is especially insightful about the rise and fall of Adolph Hitler. The lessons preached here are worthy of every thinking mind.

What I love about Eric Hoffer is his quotability. He puts ideas into such easy to remember phrases that you will find yourself quoting him off the cuff without even realizing you're doing it. Extremely well read, Mr. Hoffer is a philosopher, but also a debunker of myths. He had an uncanny ability to see straight into the heart of the matter and to dissect this information, regurgitate it and place it before the reader in such simple language that you are amazed that you didn't think of it yourself. And just what is it that Mr. Hoffer has learned, he has learned that there are repeating patterns of behavior in all mass movements that one can recognize and use to advantage. His insights will be invaluable if there ever is a mass movement in America, but according to Mr. Hoffer that is unlikely unless the middle class are forced into poverty as was the case during the Great Depression. You see, the rich like things just the way they are and the middle class are too busy struggling to keep the boat payments up to really rebel. So rebellion is of the poor, only the poor have so little to lose they are willing to rock the boat.

Mass movements follow very predictable patterns, according to Mr. Hoffer. First, they are usually fueled by the human potential of the frustrated. Those who are unable to make it in the legitimate society of the day are left to find release in the stirrings of change. Adolph Hitler, for one, was a frustrated painter; several other Nazi leaders were frustrated writers, artists and musicians. The second familiar trait of the mass movement is the need for a scapegoat on which to pour out this frustration. The Nazi's had the Jews. But almost any identifiable group will do the trick. Lastly, the mass movement must have clearly defined goals that allow the follower to fall into step without having to give anything a great deal of thought. In other words, the mass movement decides in advance what the answers are to most questions and the true believer simply follows out this belief system even if it is later proved to be absolutely ludicrous.

It is impossible to walk away from Eric Hoffer's little book and not feel that you have encountered a true soul. Whatever his reasons for remaining on the docks, I suspect he wanted to remain close to the action of the common man, he grips ideas with the eyes and mind of an intellectual bulldog. I went on to read four of Mr. Hoffer's books and found so many new quotations to use in my everyday world that I am now a bounty of new information. This may be irritating to those around me, but I am having a great time. This is the joy of being well read, you can now irritate people that have always annoyed you. And it may be said we are all potential fodder for the next mass movement. If you find yourself frustrated and tired of thinking watch out for the next slick talker you meet, he may soon have you wearing silly uniforms and gassing millions.

THE OLD MAN AND THE SEA

This short, easy read I recommend for many of the same reasons I recommended a second read by Jack Kerouac, there is something magical about seeing the world through the eyes of the very young and then seeing the world through those same eyes toward the end of the writer's life. Ernest Hemmingway published The Sun Also Rises when he was 29. He wrote The Old Man And The Sea in his fifties, less than a decade before his death. At the time The Old Man And The Sea came out Hemmingway had been through a series of literary disasters. His fine edge and terse language had disintegrated into slop. In fact Hemmingway wrote "The Old Man" while he was writing a series of less than great books about his life on the sea. Two of these books were published posthumously. In between these second rate writings this little gem had been sandwiched.

This is Hemmingway at his spare best. The language is pared down, compacted and filled with emotional intent. There is only the story. The sea, the old man, and the boat are all self-explanatory. I don't believe this book is much more than ten thousand words long and can easily be read between dinner and the start of your favorite eight o'clock television program. Yet, if one is willing, this book yields a great insight into Hemmingway and his times. The sharks can easily be interpreted as critics, critics that had been gnawing at Hemmingway for years. The old man is Earnest himself. Yet despite this obvious parallel it is possible to see the book as a metaphor for man's struggle against nature. The old man struggles, strives and finally achieves his mastery over the Marlin, only to see the poor fish devoured by sharks before he reaches port. We know that anything manmade is quickly reclaimed by nature. We only borrow our dominion for a season. On or before three million years man will almost certainly be gone, what then of all our history, all our achievements. Well, they will be swallowed up by nature her self, only to be discovered in some far distant time by archeologists from another time and place.

Hemmingway loved the outdoors and by all accounts was a staunch conservationist despite the fact that he slaughtered numerous big game animals in Africa. We must remember that in his day the supply of these exotic species seemed endless. Hemmingway lived large and died spectacularly by placing a shotgun to his chin and pulling the trigger. He is as fascinating as a man as he is as a writer. The world misses Hemmingway in the same way that the world misses any great soul. These giants cast their shadows and leave their marks then are vanished into some new world and adventure. I hope in that world I will meet up with old Ernie. He will provide ample entertainment to suffice me for an eternity.

WAR AND PEACE

After the light offering of "The Old Man" we come to the most difficult book in our arsenal. However, the rewards are all but endless if you triumph over your inaction and read and complete the masterpiece that is <u>War And Peace.</u> Depending on what edition and translation you devour the book is approximately 1443 pages long. And this, mind you, is not the Reader's Digest large print edition either. These will be tiny little words crammed about six or seven hundred on a page. So please be prepared and buy yourself a nice pair of reading glasses.

    Why this book is one of the most difficult you will soon see. First there are, according to various accounts, about three thousand characters in this book. If you have trouble figuring out who's who during the average movie, containing perhaps a dozen actors, you are in for real trouble here. But rest assured that the main characters are readily identified and some, such as Napoleon, are well known figures. The main problem comes from the way Russians talk about their pals. Suppose I give you my own name for an example, Allen Lee Scarbrough. To Tolstoy and Russians alike I might in one sentence be referred to as Allen, the next, Allen Lee, the next Allen Scarbrough, and finally in the last sentence on the page, Lee Scarbrough. So if you have three thousand characters and each name can be given to you in four different ways you now have twelve thousand names to keep track of. Rest assured when I tell you that you will fail to accomplish this. Why am I so certain, because even Tolstoy himself failed. He writes in a young woman of about nine or ten early in the book who a decade later is presented as a young woman of thirty something. It's just impossible to keep track of everyone so don't try.

Instead I recommend that you focus on the broad strokes of genius in which Russia is presented and in which the Napoleonic War is shown in all its tragic glory. When you read this book you will see not only why Russia defeated Napoleon, but also why it defeated Hitler and will likely defeat anyone else that tries to conquer it in the future. Russia is simply too vast, too cold, too protected by natural barriers and peopled with stubborn, courageous people who have no problem handling even the most extreme privation. In World War Two Hitler's armies pulverized Stalingrad into little more than a pile of rubble. Surrounded, the citizens starved, died and bled in mass. However, the Germans failed to take the city. The message is clear and simple, don't even bother to try.

War And Peace is first and foremost a compendium of Russian life, primarily among the landed and rich. The subtle interconnections between landed families and their sometimes not too subtle attempts at making advantageous matches takes us into a world that is as unfamiliar to us as ancient Rome. Russia seems to the reader as existing on another planet, a planet where feudal lords and ladies berate the masses into complying with their every wish. This book captures the attempts of Russia to become western. The way the nobility all speak French for example, and how this bold attempt fails in the short run because the masses are left behind. The peasants in this book are presented as noble, resourceful and obstinate, some are even more than a little financially independent. This is certainly due to the views of Tolstoy himself. Tolstoy believed the peasants were pure and saintly. However, many of these saintly souls had no trouble killing and maiming when given half a chance.

The pivotal era of the book is the Napoleonic War. The lessons in how Russia defended itself is a must read for any aspiring military dictator. The answer as to what to do to defend yourself from an aggressive invader? Let the poor soul have the damn place, then let him starve and freeze to death in the harsh and bitterly cold winters. Moscow was too distant from Paris for reliable supply lines to be established. The lines were too easily sabotaged and the army that had conquered Moscow had invaded a ghost town. The inhabitants had all fled. The French army burned furniture and clothing to stay warm. Upon retreating back to Paris the French burned pretty much the entire city of Moscow, yet it still stands today. On the way back a bitter and defeated Napoleon rues the day he ever heard of Russia.

Though unquestionably a long read, the book is so stuffed with historic detail, interesting characters and the lifestyles of the nineteenth century rich and famous to keep you more than amply entertained. Along the way you will also encounter moments of sheer genius, such as when the wounded officer is left on the battlefield to die and all he can see is the tranquil blue-sky overhead. I commend you in advance for making this holy literary trip with me. This book is so rewarding in terms of personal growth, but also in terms of emotional growth. And just tell a few friends that you have read this book and see what there reaction is. I assure you it will astonish and amaze them. Only professors of English read that book, or so they thought.

ONE DAY IN THE LIFE OF IVAN DENISOVICH

A rather long title for a relatively short book. Alexander Soltsynetsyn is the author of the more famous books <u>Gulag Archipelago</u> and <u>Cancer Ward</u> for which he is better known than for "Ivan" but this little treasure is chock full of life lessons that the other books simply cannot match. It is no mistake that out of these twenty-five recommended books five are from Russia. Russia is the home of literary power born out of necessity. Soltsynetsyn eventually fled Russia to live in the United States, but his Russia is the true Russia, the Russia of brutality and neglect. Ivan Denisovich is a man who has been sentenced to hard labor in the Gulags of Stalin. If the cold does not kill a man there, then surely the hard work and brutality will. Ivan strives to survive against almost impossible odds. And how does he do this? By finding self worth in his work. Ivan is a bricklayer for buildings needed by the state, and so he decides to make the most of it and find satisfaction in the positive act of construction.

What this book teaches above all is that there are things that cannot be taken from you even by the cruelest of regimes. As long as you have eyes you can view the sunset, the sunrise, the clouds, as long as you have ears you can hear the birds sing and the wind blow. And there is always the satisfaction of work. Now you may recall that earlier in this book I had you read Henry Miller and he decried most work as banal and demeaning, and so it is, but the difference here is in degree. In Miller we see the waste of excessive work, work to the point of removing oneself from the flow and ecstasy of life. In "Ivan" we see that at least some work is necessary for human survival and self esteem. So is there value in work? Absolutely, but too much is harmful to people.

What I love about this book and why I recommend it over some of Soltseytstyn's other work is that it delves into the meat of cruel environments. It takes human life on its most raw terms and deals with the consequences. Very few books have accomplished this task. Ivan Denisovich is everyman, every man who has ever lifted a brick or a bail of hay or a load of cotton or a post of lumber. Every man may find value in his life through the work that they perform, and that work keeps him from becoming mere chattel for the rich. There is also in this book an air of simplicity. Simplicity in eating, dressing, movement and speech. Everything is cut to its sparest values in order to survive the lack of sufficient food. Ivan learns that it matters not if the buildings are soon torn down, he found peace and fulfillment in the building of them and no tyrant could take this from him.

When I first read this book I was surprised to find out that although the prisoners were harshly treated there was still some manner of order among them and there was mutual respect and admiration in each man's attempt at survival. In the end the quiet dignity and nobility of the men and woman who worked on them felled the Gulag. Despite every effort being made to dehumanize and devalue them, these prisoners found a way to remain human and think and act like men. No small feat when you are outside in freezing temperatures much of the year. Soltsynetsyn is a writer of the first rank, even though he fails in comparison to the greatest Russian writers, Tolstoy and Dostoyevsky. What Soltsynetsyn accomplishes here in this little book is nothing less than the realization of the human spirit. Though we are at times a backward and stumbling species, a species that allows the coming of tyrants, we are still endowed with the spirit of goodness that bleeds out even in the worst of circumstances. Men are the inheritors of the curse of nobility. It is in our lack of capacity to measure up to this potential that the world fails men. However, men fail the world by our lack of devotion to life and respect for it as well. Men die too easily for nothing and live too easily for even less. Ivan reteaches us that to live is to yearn and hunger for a piece of the human spirit, any other way of life leads quickly to certain death, having lived an unfulfilled life.

THE ODYSSEY

This is the only example of epic poetry that I will include in this book. The Odyssey is the foremost epic poem and contains the early myths by which Greek civilization was formed. By all accounts The Odyssey was first performed orally for many decades before finally being written down more or less in the form we have it today. You can see the oral tradition in the very pattern of words Homer uses. There are many repeating phrases throughout the work, put there to aid the speaker in remembering long passages and integral connections. Homer is attributed the authorship of this work, though one wonders if it did not evolve gradually as the work of several authors and then was polished and fixed by Homer. We will likely never know.

It is impossible to be an educated and literate soul and not be familiar with the stories contained in this work. We all have heard many times the stories of the sirens that lure sailors to their deaths, the Cyclops, the enduring struggles of Odysseus as he winds his way about the Peloponnesian world striving to make it home in time before treacherous malingerers steal his wife and his fortune. Wouldn't it be nice to actually understand what people are talking about when they use these metaphors? Homer and his tale have so invaded our western thinking as to be inseparable, we envelope almost every situation in a Homeric veil.

Homer was by all accounts blind as a bat. Whether he wrote <u>The Odyssey</u> prior to or after becoming blind we do not know. He may just as well have been blind since birth. But nevertheless one need not eyes to see the beautiful and rich world that Homer creates. It is indeed a metaphorical world and not a world of flesh and blood. Even in its time (B.C.) this was a fairy tale in the highest sense of that word. But <u>The Odyssey</u> also is a bible of sorts for the Greek world that sprang up afterwards. The book acted as a sort of written pattern for Greek men to strive to attain, much as the Bible strives to teach modern men the trail to glory. Homer was in this sense a prophet, though he predicted not specific events so much as the entire pattern of human existence for nearly all of time.

Is this giving Homer too much credit? Did he really reveal so much about human nature that we can ascribe to him the title of prophet, yep, we can. Homer "sees" in ways the average man cannot and his blindness acts as a catalyst (supposing that the blindness occurred before the book) to viewing the world in a way so unfamiliar to the men of the time as to act as a pattern for the future. Not a pattern for men to follow, but a pattern which men must trod even if they wish otherwise because that is their nature and will be for millennium to come.

Western civilization can be said to have sprung from the Greeks. Even the Romans struggled to emulate the Greeks whose intellectual accomplishments far out shadowed the paltry output of Rome. When we speak of philosophy we immediately think of Plato and Aristotle, when we think of plays we think of Sophocles, Aristophanes, and Euripides. When we think of mathematicians we think of Euclid and Pythagoras. All that we have striven to be in the west has been founded on the cradle of Greece. And of all these great men and their great ideas Homer stands at the head of the table and lends to all of them their true value in the history of the world. Homer is the Shakespeare of the Greeks, the Isaiah of the Greeks, and the Tolstoy of the Greeks. To know Homer is to know almost everything about human beings.

I will have to admit that it is difficult to absorb everything this book has to offer in one reading, so on this one book I offer a suggestion. After reading the book I want you to find an audiotape or CD of it in your public library and listen to it for a second reading. Because The Odyssey was indeed an oral story, told for countless years in streets and alleyways it lends itself deliciously to a hearing as well as a reading. If you are like me I enjoyed the oral version even better, and let's face it everybody likes a good bedtime story told by a master storyteller in a deep rich voice that transports you to another time and place. I imagine nobody did this better than Homer, he is a gift to all generations and so is his masterpiece.

ANNA KARININA

This is Tolstoy's second masterpiece and fits very easily into any-one's (anyone with a brain that is) top five novels of all time list. I rank it third, but that's just me. This book is important not only for its understanding and insight into the Russia that once existed, but for its equally towering insight into the plight of women in patriar-chal societies. This is the tale of a woman told by a man, but done so with such grace and dignity so as not to offend the fairer sex. After wading through the character minefield that is <u>War and Peace</u> you should now be quite familiar with the peculiarities of Russian litera-ture, so this should be a much easier read, and I should say much shorter, only bout half the 1443 pages of that monstrous tome pre-viously mentioned. I found this book so enthralling that I stayed up all one Saturday night to finish it. Starting from page 344 I made it to the end, page 844 by sunrise, I couldn't see for three days how-ever.

Some of the grandest and noblest insights into human nature are presented in this work. In many subtle ways this book surpasses even <u>War and Peace</u> in scope and insight. For the females in my reading audience this book will probably make you angry at times, please do not take out your anger on your husbands and boyfriends, they know not what they do. The anger comes from the avenues society shuts off from women, especially woman who cheat on their husbands. Yes, the main character is an adulterer, but that makes her different from most men how?

Anna is a woman of the modern sense, who lives in a time when that is still a vile word. The old world is crumbling, yes, but not so fast as she would like. Anna must walk a tightrope between the social station and wealth provided by her husband, though not much love and intimacy, or the passion and love she feels for her lover, Count Vronsky. Many, many men have been portrayed in literature in this exact situation but this is arguably the first example of a woman doing so. Anna eventually suffers for her crime and is exiled from society. She has paid a dear price for her social insolence.

When this book was written, during Tolstoy's prime, the world of Russia was at a crossroads. The stirrings of change would ultimately lead to the revolution of the early twentieth century. Russia has always been a country balanced on the edge of east and west and has never found total comfort in either place. Russian women of the eighteen hundred's were held to a double standard, which is most of Tolstoy's point. This has not changed even in our time and will not likely change for another hundred years. I need to say little about this book really. No one could dispute its importance, its influence or its worth. This book will stay with you on long lonely winter nights, exactly the intent of old Leo himself.

THE ART OF WAR

This book is all the rage these days. I found it high on the sales list at Amazon.com. It was featured in the eighties movie about greed "Wall Street" and is Gecco's, the main character and corporate raider, code of conduct. A warrior named Sun Tzu wrote it. By all accounts he was a wise man who fought battles for royalty and was well respected for his strategies. It is rumored that he was once challenged to turn the prince's handmaids into an army. At first he spoke a command and was not obeyed. He calmly walked over to the first handmaid whipped out his sword and smote off her head. He issued another order, this time he was obeyed. Point, set, match to Sun Tzu.

The reason I am so adamant that any thinking man or woman should read this book is the deep insight into eastern social thinking that it reveals. Do not go into negotiations with a Japanese or Chinese firm without first reading The Art Of War. That would be like going into a nest of vipers with no clothes on. The east thinks holistically, not only in warfare but also in business, politics and life in general. Business in the east is warfare and it is perfectly okay to spy, steal or pry information out of the west. Seemingly hapless Japanese, only "asking questions," have duped America out of many of its top engineering secrets. Talkers beware.

This book is used today as much as it ever was because it does not focus on the implements of war, such as swords and horses, but on the overlying strategy of war. Horses have become tanks, and swords have become laser guided missiles, but the tactics of warfare will not change. The man with the best plan who gets to the area first with the most firepower wins. That is the strategy of war in a nutshell. It has been working for thousands of years. But make no mistake Napoleon or General Lee did not invent it, Sun Tzu was aware of this fact long before America or France was ever born. I suspect also that Sun Tzu had a lot of time on his hands. After all, how would he have written this book if he had been busy fighting battles all day?

The beauty of Sun Tzu is the universality of his work. The basic strategic principles, such as divide and conquer, can be used to defeat a foe in business or politics, or even a rival for a lover's affections. It can even be used on Wall Street though I do not believe Sun Tzu ever said "greed is good." Greed is stupid and Sun Tzu was well aware of that fact. In actuality his strategies are so subtle in some cases as to not be strategies at all, but more modes of action. We in the west dissect and probe, in the east they penetrate and absorb. So I'm not sure to what extent Sun Tzu would have been followed in this country. However, he is gaining a miraculous following for the reasons that strategy is strategy and everyone in the west is always looking to gain an upper hand, which unfortunately is the exact opposite of Sun Tzu's principles of war, but we probably aren't going to learn this anytime soon. Read and be reborn as a warrior.

EAST OF EDEN

Again I return my attention to John Steinbeck. Though it is still being debated in some circles as to how great a writer he was I will simply move on and promise you that he was. Refer back to the former section on <u>The Grapes Of Wrath</u> if you need to refresh your memory as to what I previously said about him. The importance of Steinbeck for our purposes is his sweeping epic vision of America during some of the most critical points in our development. In one book it is the great depression, in this book it is the settling of the west. Both eras reveal great truths about ourselves that no thinking man or woman will want to ignore.

In essence <u>East Of Eden</u> is a modern retelling of the story of Cain and Abel. Two brothers compete for the love of their father and the results are tragic. Though many of you will have seen one or more of the movie versions of this work rest assured that much of the meat has been trimmed to fit a two-hour time slot. This book is a long, rambunctious ride. From the farmland of Salinas to whorehouses, to railroad cars carrying lettuce across the country this story is as sweeping in scope as America itself. Steinbeck was ultimately an American who wrote about the faults of America yet with admiration for his country.

What I found in Steinbeck that perhaps others have not is a wise old soul. Any flaws in his books can be overlooked for the poignancy and depth of his feeling for the subjects he writes about. Particularly you can see this in the novella <u>Of Mice And Men,</u> a book I also highly recommend. It is Steinbeck's love of his characters that bleeds through the pages and leaps into the reader's imagination. Because of this fact Steinbeck's characters seem to take on a life of their own. Dozens of actors in Hollywood have hungered to play the role of the retarded Lenny. <u>East Of Eden</u> attracted James Dean himself in a role that can never be exceeded in depth and power. Steinbeck's characters breathe and work and play and feel and he makes you understand this in a profound way. There have been many great characters created in the history of literature and Steinbeck created more than his fair share of them.

And just what is it that Steinbeck is saying about America. I think he is saying that America is an evolving experiment, flawed yet beautiful. The Constitution did not secure all rights for all people; it was not a perfect document straight from the mouth of deity. The Constitution, and the country it supports, is a dynamic evolving social contract, and it needs polishing from time to time. Remember that most of the freedoms and privileges we enjoy were a part of The Bill Of Rights, all these freedoms were missing from the Constitution itself. Steinbeck sees this as the great power of our land, the ability to reinvent us as circumstances dictate. Certainly in the Great Depression, many of our basic tenets of democracy were called into question. Constant probing, according to Steinbeck's works, is a necessary function of democracy.

Getting back to the story, <u>East Of Eden</u> is Steinbeck's attempt to bring Old Testament teachings in line with the assaults upon it by philosophers and critics. In short the book is an exploration of the age-old question, one never fully answered as yet by anyone, as to how a just and perfect God creates evil and allows his creatures to go to hell for all eternity. Steinbeck doesn't really answer the question so much as he offers another explanation. Steinbeck gives us a new understanding that man "mayest" return to God, in other words man brought evil into the world through the fall and man is endowed with the free will to return into God's presence if he is obedient. Free will then is the reason we have pain and suffering and hunger in the world. I think this is utter bunk, but it is a better explanation than that God created both good and evil. If God can create evil He is not all good.

I still cherish the hours I spent in Steinbeck's company, meeting the man through his words that live on after him. I found Steinbeck to be a warm and reassuring figure that loved deeply and well and wanted more than anything to find a way for man to escape his own nature. Who knows what John thought toward the end of his life, he may have secretly given up on the whole idea, then again maybe he found an answer he never got around to telling us.

A SAND COUNTY
ALMANAC

I introduce you now to some of the best nature writing the world has ever seen. <u>Walden</u>, to me, is a book about man's relationship to nature and surely it is a great work of literature, but Aldo Leopold's <u>A Sand County Almanac</u> is concerned with an appreciation of what exists out in nature for man to discover. This book was a complete revelation to me when I first read it eighteen years ago. I still think of the deep, penetrating insights into the life of Sand County that Aldo portrays. This book "sticks to your ribs" as they say. I think about it often even though it contains no human characters or any discernable story. The story in this book is nature itself, nature going about its business with or without the intervention of man. The areas that Aldo writes about seem as busy and alive as any superhighway and the abundance and vitality of the creatures contained in it still mesmerize me to this day.

What I have always believed concerned Leopold is the acceptance by men that nature can get along fine without him, that the world was here long before the intervention of man, or even the creation of man. Life simply evolves in ever more complex circles and perhaps intelligent life evolves with it or perhaps it does not. The rich textures of this book indicate that if a man is willing and focuses enough of his attention he may begin to see the beauty and subtlety of what he normally dismisses as crude nature. In our time, long after the writing of <u>A Sand County Almanac</u>, we have the ability to see with long range, and stop-time photography, the delicate world that lives under our noses with astonishing detail. This is what Aldo Leopold was trying to teach us so many years ago and simply did not possess the technology to show us first hand.

In this book an entire tiny universe is captured in a fleeting moment that lives on in your mind for years to come. It is impossible to look the same way again at an acre or two of land. After you read this book that small parcel of soil will have become in your mind a separate world capable of existence without assistance or interference. Life is fragile in many ways, but it is also intricately interconnected and life finds a way to survive even the harshest of climates. Aldo Leopold is in my mind the first great explorer of these worlds and certainly the first one to write about it in such forceful language that readers decades later still marvel at what he shows. This book can be read easily in one sitting if one has the wherewithal to invest about three hours of continuous time. I strongly urge you to read it in one sitting if at all possible. That way the force and power of Sand County will appear to you much like a dream, because in the end it is a great dream, the dream of the future, a future man will destroy if he is not careful. And man is rarely careful.

A BRIEF HISTORY OF TIME

In reality I could have listed any of a hundred books here in this final slot. I chose this one because I felt that at least one book on the current state of physics is necessary to developing any well rounded individual. There is so much talk in the news today about all the new findings, new theories, old theories overthrown, and plain old speculation that it is now necessary to at least own a scorecard on what's going on. I chose <u>A Brief History Of Time,</u> even though I like other books on the same subject better, because the greatest living Physicist, Stephen Hawking, writes it in plain English with little or no math. Hawking himself is a very interesting man. Crippled by MS he contemplates the universe from a wheel chair communicating via an electronic voice synthesizer.

This is also a book that is easy to obtain, a short read, and is clear and concise. I must warn you in advance that if you find the subject matter at all interesting you might find yourself immersed in the subjects Hawking presents. There are literally hundreds of current books available on the current state of our understanding of the universe. I have read them all. This is my subject; I love to read these types of books above all others. But Hawking's little book is an excellent place to start for the uninitiated or the marginally knowledgeable. Stephen Hawking is to this date the only man to have presented a theory that in any way unites the Theory Of Relativity with Quantum Mechanics. His discovery that black holes radiate energy is his highest achievement to date. If you have no idea what I just said then please read this book extra carefully.

As our technology gets ever more precise our ability to directly observe natural phenomena increases exponentially. In the future we may be able to peer all the way back to the opaque barrier that existed, and sheltered the universe from light, until about 300,000 after the Big Bang. What happened in that first 300,000 years we are never likely to experience directly, but we will through mathematics be able to understand what happened and why. What we are waiting for is a Theory Of Everything, a theory that will unite the four known forces of nature into one and reveal at last the physics that existed in the first 10 to the negative 43rd power of a second. Then we will have a complete description of all of nature and all phenomena that exists in it. What's the hold up? Gravity. Gravity is the monster we cannot seem to grasp. According to Einstein gravity is the curvature of space-time in the presence of matter or energy, matter and energy being different aspects of the same thing, this theory has worked brilliantly through the years and has been verified by so many experiments they are too numerous to mention. Rest assured that the basic tenets of Relativity are correct. But when we peer into the smallest possible spaces and in the light of so many new discoveries involving Quantum Mechanics gravity seems at odds with everything else. Can nature be so two-faced? Not likely, so an even better description of gravity, one that unites it to the other known forces is needed.

There are at this writing several candidates for this theory, among them are String Theory, Superstring Theory, M-Theory, and Quantum Loop Gravity, a personal favorite of mine because it states that space and time are discrete at the most fundamental level, a hypothesis I am certain is correct. Nevertheless, no theory has proven to work in all circumstances and under close inspection. All of these theories fall short in one way or another. It is predicted that within fifty years we will have in our possession a complete description of nature and the rest as Einstein said is "just details."

The nature of the universe is important to understand for all endeavors of life. We will end hunger and discover unlimited supplies of energy and finally and at last colonize mars once this important discovery of The Theory Of Everything is complete. Though it is unlikely that we will make this discovery during Stephan Hawking's lifetime it is certain that he would have understood it and what's even more important he would have made you and I understand it. In this vein Hawking was probably born thirty years too early, unless of course another person with Hawking's ability to communicate looms on the horizon. I sincerely hope so. May the Theory Of Everything bring us peace and prosperity. Amen.

GRADUATION DAY

We have now completed our one-year (okay, for some it was slightly longer) program of self-education. If you have followed this program dutifully you are even as we speak irritating your friends and neighbors with all your "high mightiness and haughty learning." It feels great doesn't it? Now you can leave your undereducated friends behind and find new sources of human amusement. But seriously, if you have faithfully followed the outline of this book you have come into possession of some of the greatest learning it is possible to receive. You, my friend, are among the elite, the educated, the possessors of light and truth. Now go forth and change the world, it needs it.

P.S. Your receipt for this book is your actual diploma. Congratulations!!!!!

0-595-24315-0